Let's Learn About...
LLAMAS
By: Breanne Sartori

All Rights Reserved. No part of this publication may be reproduced in any form or by any means, including scanning, photocopying, or otherwise without prior written permission of the copyright holder. Copyright © 2014

Introduction

Llamas are funny looking animals that are well known for their tendency to spit! Even though their faces sometimes look a bit dopey they are actually very intelligent animals! Most llamas have been domesticated, but there are still some in the wild. They are actually one of the oldest domesticated animals in the world!

What is a Llama

Can you guess what type of animals llamas are related to? They're related to camels! It is thought that camels and llamas descended from the same animal a long time ago. Even though they are part of the camel family, they have evolved to be very different because of the environment they live in!

What Llamas Look Like

Llamas are tall animals with big bodies and long, thin necks. Their heads are quite small compared to their body. Their faces look a lot like a sheep or goat and so does their wool. Llamas walk on four, thin legs which are also covered in fur. They have a small, shaggy tail too!

Wool

The wool of a llama doesn't look like it would be very soft, but it is! It is one of the warmest and lightest wools out of all animals and is very popular for making blankets, jumpers and scarves. The wool comes in all sorts of colours – brown, grey, black, white, red and yellow. Not only is it nice and soft, it's also fireproof!

Feet

Llama feet have two toes each. They are spread wide to help them walk through tricky terrain. The bottom of their feet are soft and padded which stop them slipping when they walk.

Where Llamas Live

Llamas live in South America, mainly Peru, Ecuador and Bolivia. They once used to live in North America too, but are now extinct there. They live in the Andes mountain ranges in grasslands and deserts.

What Llamas Eat

Llamas are herbivores and their favourite food is grass. They can eat a lot of different types of plants though. Domesticated llamas can even survive eating hay! Llamas are grazing animals, so they spend a lot of time eating!

Rumination

Like other grazing animals, llamas are ruminants. This means that they regurgitate their food so that they can chew it again! Once they have chewed this (it's called "cud") they swallow it and it digests completely. Llamas have three sections in their stomach which allows this to happen.

Drinking

Llamas don't need to drink very much, which is lucky because water is hard to come by where they live. Most of the water they need to live on they get from the plants that they eat. They still need to drink when they can though.

Social Life

Llamas are really social animals! They live in herds and hate being apart from each other. Even so they are quite shy animals and will act independently. They are also really curious and gentle, so they get along with humans really well – even children!

Herd

Everyone in the herd has their place, but this can easily be disrupted! Instead of the strongest llama being the leader of the herd, it's the most disciplined! The llamas who are most naughty are at the bottom of the social ladder. The rank of llamas can change pretty suddenly – especially when fights break out!

Communication

A lot of the time llamas communicate with their bodies. The way they hold their tail or ears signals to other llamas how they are feeling. When in danger they will make a call that sounds like an alarm and they hum when they want to show affection.

Domestication

Llamas and alpacas aren't really wild animals anymore – they've been domesticated just like sheep. They are used by people to help carry things because they are very tough and strong. The ancient people of the Inca culture in Peru first domesticated them centuries ago to use them for their wool, meat and to carry things.

Baby Llamas

Baby llamas are called cria. They are born live and will be walking around and nursing within 90 minutes of being born! Strangely, llama babies are most often born in the morning! Some people think this is because the weather is warmer then.

Breeding

Llamas will breed any time of year. When the female gives birth, she does so standing up. Other female llamas will form a circle around her to protect the newborn from male llamas and predators. Even though llamas can breed any time of year, they can still only give birth one a year because they are pregnant for about 11 months!

The Life of a Llama

After about 6 months the cria no longer need to rely on their mother's milk. Instead they can start grazing like the adults. When they are about 18 months old they are old enough to start breeding and will have their first baby when they are two and a half. Llama can live to be 20 years old.

Predators

The main predators of llamas are pumas and cougars. Because many of them no longer live in the wild they don't have to worry about them too much. Most are killed by humans who farm them for their meat and skin!

Defending Themselves

Llamas don't have any weapons that they can use to defend themselves. But if you make one angry, prepare to be spat on! Instead of biting, llamas choose to spit at animals and humans that annoy them instead!

Alpaca

It can be very difficult to tell the difference between a llama and an alpaca. They look very similar and they are both domesticated for their wool and meat. They are smaller and woolier than llamas though. This breed is used only for their wool and meat, they aren't pack animals.

Vicuna

The wool of a vicuna is very expensive! This is because their wool is of very good quality and the animal can only be shaved every three years! The vicuna looks more like a deer than the other species of llama and are the smallest species. Some are domesticated, but they are mostly wild.

Guanaco

The guanaco is a wild species of llama that has short hair. They actually have two layers of hair – the soft undercoat and a rough coat on top called a "guard coat". The guanaco is found very far south in Chile and Argentina but they aren't very numerous and are considered endangered.

Made in the USA
San Bernardino, CA
06 March 2017